SPORTS AND ENTERTAINMENT MARKETING

MINI-SIMULATIONS

Kay Masonbrink
Rancho Bernardo High School
San Diego, CA

Betty Sellers
Marketing Consultant
San Diego, CA

 **Glencoe McGraw-Hill**

New York, New York   Columbus, Ohio   Woodland Hills, California   Peoria, Illinois

Glencoe/McGraw-Hill

A Division of The McGraw·Hill Companies

Printed in the United States of America.

Send all inquiries to:
Glencoe/McGraw-Hill
21600 Oxnard St. Suite 500
Woodland Hills, California 91367-4906

ISBN 0-07-824956-2

1 2 3 4 5 6 7 8 9   009   06 05 04 03 02 01

SPORTS AND
ENTERTAINMENT
MARKETING

TABLE OF CONTENTS

SPORTS AND
ENTERTAINMENT
MARKETING

WELCOME TO IMPACT! INC.

Impact! Inc. is a leading provider of innovative sports and entertainment marketing services throughout the United States. The owners are a former professional tennis player and a former director of marketing at a Hollywood movie studio. They met while working on a promotional campaign and quickly learned of their shared desire to be in business for themselves. They were eager to form a marketing firm that took advantage of their combined knowledge of sports and entertainment. After researching the marketing field, they discovered that there is ample opportunity in the sports and entertainment segment. Their partnership was born to fill a void for sports and entertainment-related clients looking to achieve specific marketing needs that work in conjunction with their advertising messages.

Today, Impact! Inc. is a full-service marketing agency with a talented staff of over 80 marketing professionals. The agency is dedicated to developing concepts that provide measurable media value and delivering clients' messages to the appropriate audiences via promotional announcements and advertisements.

Services

Impact! Inc. offers a wide range of marketing services:

- ◆ Advertising—Clear messages, proven results.
- ◆ Campaign Development—Customized campaigns to reinforce the advertising messages.
- ◆ Consultation—Pricing and distribution.
- ◆ Full-Service Art Department—Concept, design, art direction, and production management.
- ◆ Market Research and Evaluation—Tracking the competition, evaluating the market, and achieving results.
- ◆ Packaging/Branding—Defining product identity.
- ◆ Personal Selling—Customized one-on-one presentations.
- ◆ Product Development—Introducing new products and modernizing and re-introducing existing products.
- ◆ Publicity and Public Relations—Handle difficult situations during difficult times, provide strong media contacts, supply unequaled client exposure.
- ◆ Sales Promotion—Trade shows, licensing, promotional tie-ins, merchandising, and incentives.

Your Role and Job Responsibilities

Congratulations! You have been selected to join the Impact! Inc. training program! As a trainee, you'll be working in several different departments and be responsible for a wide variety of marketing tasks. The goals of the trainee program are to expose you to as much of the overall promotional mix as possible and to give you first-hand experience using the skills and situations necessary to succeed in sports and entertainment marketing. You'll find that your duties inevitably revolve around the four Ps of marketing: product, place, price, and promotion. Your knowledge of entrepreneurial concepts and selling skills will also help you in this endeavor.

Impact! Inc. has developed and executed campaigns for many national and international clients. We have developed a reputation of honesty and respectability with these clients and expect you to continue in that tradition. You will be working with several clients, including

◆ Old Tyme Toys
◆ Masters Shoe Company
◆ OK Wood
◆ Torrel Dance Troupe
◆ Palmer Bicycle Company
◆ Performances to Please
◆ Venture Group Limited

You will be given background files for each assignment. As you move between accounts and through the different Impact! Inc. departments, we expect you to manage your time wisely and submit your assignments in an organized fashion. *Do your best and be creative!*

SPORTS AND ENTERTAINMENT MARKETING

BACKGROUND FILE

SIMULATION 1
CLIENT: Old Tyme Toy Company
CLASSIFICATION: Toy Manufacturer

CLIENT BACKGROUND

It's hard to find a kid in America who isn't familiar with the products of Old Tyme. The toy company that brought the world DinoMite!—The Dinosaur Board Game—is proudly celebrating its fiftieth year in the toy business. Any industry insider, however, will tell you that Old Tyme's beginnings in the toy business were nothing to celebrate. The company began as a small family-owned business offering just a few products including a line of playing cards and a couple of unsuccessful board games. In an attempt to expand its product line, the family gambled on a risky product: the stringless yo-yo. It was a miserable failure that left the family nearly bankrupt. In a desperate and final effort to pull itself out of debt, the family decided to capitalize on the popularity of "Jacks" with a product called "Tacks." Another major setback, the product sold poorly, and children complained that they "hurt to pick up." Soon after the release of "Tacks," the family was forced to sell the company to Nigel Wright, a savvy investor who was able to turn Old Tyme around.

In the late 1960s and throughout the 1970s, the Old Tyme Toy Company could do no wrong. Mr. Wright released hit toy after hit toy culminating with the enormously popular Lettuce Babies in the mid-1980s. The company's jingle said it all: "Good Times begin with Old Tymes!"

Lately, however, it seems that Old Tyme has fallen on hard times. A recent report indicates a significant decline in sales of several classic toys. The Old Tyme management refuses to drop the items that help put the company on top. Instead, it has decided to update and redesign the "classics" line and pump new life into its other products.

ASSIGNMENT

Old Tyme has contracted the entertainment division of Impact! Inc. to assist in the modernization cycle of its older products and re-introduce them to the consumer. We will work closely with Lisa McCallum, Old Tyme's Senior Vice-President of Product Development. She will oversee all aspects of the "50th Anniversary Relaunch," focusing on five classic products:

Big Haul Tractor—push truck for the sandbox or playing in the dirt (ages 3-10).

DinoMite!—dinosaur board game (ages 3-8).

E-Z Erector Set—building system for constructive play without nuts or bolts (ages 6-10).

Lettuce Babies—cloth dolls with distinctive round faces, colorful clothing and frameable birth certificates (ages 3 and up).

Speedway—slot-car race set with track (ages 6-12).

Drop what you're doing and focus your attention on the Old Tyme account. Pick the toy that strikes your fancy and get started!

PHASE I PRODUCT DEVELOPMENT

Now that you've selected an Old Tyme toy, you need to do some good old-fashioned research and development (R&D). Lisa insists that you firmly adhere to the "six-step process of new product development." That means (1) generating the idea, (2) screening ideas, (3) developing the product, (4) testing the product, (5) introducing the product, and (6) evaluating customer acceptance. With this in mind, proceed as follows:

STEP 1

Generate ideas on how to modify and/or redesign your toy to improve consumer appeal and increase revenue. Identify the ways in which you generated these new ideas. (What inspired you?) Then spell out the role technology has played in the demise of your Old Tyme toy.

_____

_____

_____

_____

_____

STEP 2

It wouldn't be R&D without screening. Evaluate your ideas and identify the factors you considered.

_____

_____

_____

_____

_____

_____

_____

STEP 3

After the screening process, develop the product. Provide a detailed description for building and testing an accurate prototype.

_____

_____

_____

_____

STEP 4

While it may seem like overkill, it's important to test at least five aspects of the toy. Identify various consumer testing methodologies and the methodology you would choose to test the feasability of the new toy. Prepare a feasability testing question-naire with questions regarding the product line extension.

_____

_____

_____

_____

STEP 5

Decide how to introduce and publicize the product. Raising the public's interest and excitement will increase the feasibility of Old Tyme's investment in your product.

_____

_____

_____

STEP 6

Plan how to evaluate customer acceptance of the product. What will necessitate Old Tyme's extension of the product line? Justify your answer.

_____

_____

_____

PHASE 2 PACKAGING

Now the fun part, packaging! This is an area where Old Tyme reallyneeds help.

STEP 1

Since the "Tacks" fiasco, safety is at the forefront of Old Tyme's product development list. Identify the safety considerations for creating your toy's packaging. What must appear on the package itself? Some examples include small part warnings, electrical warnings, breakable parts, plastic bags, etc.

_____

_____

_____

_____

STEP 2

Old Tyme is a long-time leader in the movement toward environmentally sound packaging. How will this affect your packaging recommendations? First, head to the library or research online to find out the types of recyclable materials available for packaging. Also, decide if the package copy should indicate if it is made from post-recycled products. Why or why not?

_____

_____

_____

_____

STEP 3

Lisa says that the distribution process has hurt sales on more poorly packaged products. (There's nothing worse than a kid opening up a broken toy!) Knowing this, describe how the package will protect the toy during distribution. (Remember the package must be easy to open.)

_____

_____

_____

_____

STEP 4

Create your own mock-up for the packaging of your newly-designed Old Tyme toy. It is best to do this using desktop publishing or illustration software, but if that is unavailable, use the box below or a separate sheet of paper. Below the artwork, indicate all of the necessary elements of your proposed packaging and how each will influence the buyer. Be sure to include your package's physical appearance (size, shape, color, materials), labeling (title, age indicators, directions) and branding (brand name, mark, trademark, licensing, etc.).

STEP 5

Finally, outline a "directions for use" sheet to enclose inside the package. Indicate the diagrams and explanations to include. Prepare a mock-up version using a desktop publishing program, or sketch one in the box below or on a separate sheet of paper.

PHASE 3 | EXPANSION

STEP 1

Lisa phoned this morning to request sales projections for her meeting with Mr. Wright next week. While sales of your toy have been declining recently, it has a history of generating from 3 percent to 14 percent of Old Tyme's total sales (see chart below). Using these numbers, and either a spreadsheet program or the printout below, calculate the following:

A. The revenue your toy will produce at the 3, 5, 8, 11, and 14 percent levels for each of the five years.

YEAR	OLD TYME PROJECTED TOTAL SALES	3%	5%	8%	11%	14%
1	$30,000,000					
2	$32,000,000					
3	$34,000,000					
4	$36,000,000					
5	$38,000,000					

B. Assuming the Year 2 projected sales were low and actual sales were closer to $32,600,000, how much more in sales must your toy generate to maintain the charted percentages?

YEAR	OLD TYME PROJECTED TOTAL SALES	3%	5%	8%	11%	14%
2	$32,600,000					

C. It's not uncommon for 60 percent of all toy sales to occur between the months of October and December due to the holidays. Assuming this, what must the average monthly sales projections be for the previous months of the year? How will you modify your Old Tyme toy, or extend the line to generate more sales from January through September?

_____

_____

 _____

STEP 2

A fax from Old Tyme yesterday requests your thoughts on international sales. Identify the country that suits your product, and list any considerations you feel Old Tyme must make to market the product successfully. Include packaging modifications, if necessary.

_____

_____

_____

STEP 3

Old Tyme's CEO Nigel Wright wants to increase Old Tyme's involvement in the industrial market. Describe below the key differences between the consumer and industrial toy markets. Then brainstorm and list five ways Old Tyme can expand your toy's use to appeal to an industrial setting. (For example, Old Tyme could sell dolls to day care centers or hospitals.) If your ideas are good, they could open up a big chunk of new business for Impact! Inc.

_____

_____

_____

STEP 4

Speaking of new business, take the lead and try to broaden the scope of Impact! Inc.'s account work with Old Tyme. Summarize the advantages and disadvantages of a single product vs. a product line. Then, using your Old Tyme toy, identify ways of extending it into a product line.

_____

_____

_____

STEP 5

Old Tyme never includes mail-in warranty cards in its packaging. Write a paragraph detailing the advantages of doing so. Then create a warranty card including a customer satisfaction survey for packaging with your Old Tyme toy.

_____

_____

_____

_____

SPORTS AND
ENTERTAINMENT
MARKETING

SIMULATION 2

CLIENT: Masters Shoe Company

CLASSIFICATION: Soccer Shoe Manufacturer

CLIENT BACKGROUND

For more than 30 years, the Masters Company has manufactured fashionable, comfortable, and durable golf shoes. The company took a leadership role in the golf equipment industry by developing new materials to extend the life of the shoe spike. Molded into the sole of the shoe to provide maximum comfort and safety, the new plastic spikes are virtually indestructible. Along with excellent reviews, sales of the new Masters golf shoe have climbed 13 percent over last year.

Charlene Park is the product manager of Masters Shoe Company. After winning soccer championships as a player in North American youth leagues, American collegiate competition, and European pro leagues, she returned to the United States to join Masters as a product manager. Charlene was impressed with Masters' dedication to producing quality shoes, and recognized enormous potential in expanding Masters' product line. If Masters can make a soccer shoe as good as its golf shoe, she thought, it could rule the market for soccer shoes as well. The introduction of the new golf spike was just the ammunition Charlene needed to convince Masters to launch a line of soccer shoes.

Without question, soccer is the most popular sport in the world, and since America hosted the World Cup in 1994, its popularity in the United States has skyrocketed. Youth soccer leagues even challenge baseball little leagues in popularity across the U.S., with pro leagues gaining mainstream attention. This new soccer-mania, coupled with the success of Masters' new spike, led the company to develop and market a soccer shoe in both children's and adult sizes.

Product testing shows the shoes to be lightweight and supple. They provide a close feel for the ball and clearly surpass all other shoes for durability. Market research reveals

continued on next page

ASSIGNMENT

Impact! Inc. has just inked the deal with Masters to develop the most effective distribution system for the new soccer shoe line. This involves research, evaluation and ultimately, recommendations. Masters' goal is to achieve the highest possible market penetration as quickly as possible (before other manufacturers begin developing and marketing the new spike technology).

Oh, and just so you know, the president of Impact! Inc. is an old college buddy of Charlene's. Needless to say, your performance is going to be put under a microscope.

CLIENT BACKGROUND *(continued)*

that, as with the Masters golf shoe, consumers will pay a higher price for soccer shoes that will go the distance.

The shoe's target market is male and female soccer players of all ages. Charlene's market research indicates that $100 is a strong price point in the soccer shoe market, but because of Masters' extended wear factor, the shoes will be priced at $125.

Deciding how to get the shoes to consumers, however, is not so simple. It has always been Masters' practice to sell its golf shoes using an indirect and somewhat exclusive channel. As a result, they have not been widely carried in the larger sporting goods chains and discount stores. Instead, Masters maintains a small sales force and uses manufacturer's reps to call on, promote, and sell the shoes to pro shops and specialty golf stores for resale. The reps then send their orders to Masters for shipping directly to the stores. Masters bills the retailers direct and pays the reps a 7 percent commission.

Masters' distribution system works extremely well for its golf shoes. Charlene wants to develop a new system for the soccer shoes, however, including new locations and methods to make the product more available for the target consumer. And she wants Impact! Inc. to help.

PHASE I RESEARCH

Before making any recommendations, you need to dive into the soccer shoe marketplace and soak up as much information as you can about Masters' competitors' distribution channels. This information exists in books and periodicals, online, or through personal interviews. Here are some leads:

BOOKS

Check historical accounts of competitive companies. *Swoosh: The Unauthorized Story of Nike and the Men Who Played There* comes to mind.

PERIODICALS

Head over to the library when you get a break, and bury yourself in the Reader's Guide to Periodicals. You'll find a bunch of stuff on the competition: Adidas, Nike, etc.

ONLINE

Surf the Net to locate competitive Web sites. You can search under the shoe companies' names or enter "soccer shoes" as key words.

INTERVIEWS

Drop by a few of the local sporting goods stores or call some corporate toll-free numbers to pick the brains of representatives about their distribution channels.

All of these resources will help you learn about the distribution channels other shoe companies use. Organize these channels by manufacturer, and indicate on the following chart, or on a separate sheet of paper, how successful they are. Prepare a written summary in chart form of your findings to use in an oral presentation to the rest of the staff to get their approval.

See Chart Next Page

MANUFACTURER	DISTRIBUTION CHANNEL	SUCCESS

STEP 1

Now that you know what the competition is up to, use the table below to supply Masters with a complete list of all possible distribution channels and the benefits and drawbacks of each. Be sure to include issues of control, costs, terms, international market connections, and multiple channels.

DISTRIBUTION CHANNEL MEMBERS	BENEFITS	DRAWBACKS

STEP 2

An e-mail from Charlene's assistant requests your thoughts on distribution intensity for the new Masters soccer shoe line.

A. Define the three levels of distribution intensity: intensive, exclusive, and selective.

_____

_____

_____

_____

_____

_____

_____

B. Indicate the most appropriate level for Masters soccer shoes, and why.

_____

_____

_____

_____

_____

_____

_____

_____

_____

_____

C. Based on the distribution intensity, create a database of at least 20 stores or outlets that will potentially carry Masters soccer shoes. (Locate these names using online research, directories, personal visits, etc.) Design the database using information necessary for Masters to develop an association with its prospects: name, address, phone number, fax number, e-mail, name of store buyer, products carried, and so on. Use a database application to perform this activity, or create it on a separate sheet of paper.

STEP 3

Masters' current method of direct distribution involves the following steps:

1. Determine promotional plan to reach market.
   - ◆ Advertising
   - ◆ Publicity
   - ◆ Personal Selling (Internet, direct mail, catalogs, sales force, toll-free number, etc.)
   - ◆ Sales promotion activities
2. Create order-taking/processing system.
3. Create billing/invoice system with credit terms.
4. Establish return/adjustment procedures.
5. Establish inventory control for raw materials and finished product.
6. Develop shipping procedures (space, personnel, cost, time, methods).
7. Warehousing, physical space considerations.

If all goes well with the soccer shoe introduction, Charlene will propose a plan to Masters for a series of retail stores under the Masters Foot Wear name. Her first concern, however, is what, if any, conflicts the Masters retail outlets will face if they enter the retail business. Address this concern below.

_____

_____

_____

_____

_____

_____

_____

_____

_____

_____

_____

_____

_____

The Impact! president ran into Charlene in the lobby yesterday. After reminiscing about their college days, they discussed the progress on the Masters account. Charlene was pleased, but the president walked away feeling a little out of the loop. As a result, you must give an oral presentation of your findings and recommendations to the entire staff. It's important to make a good impression, so organize your thoughts well, and speak clearly. Also, be sure to cover the following topics:

◆ What the competition is doing
◆ Options for distribution channels
◆ Options for distribution intensity
◆ Your recommendation

SPORTS AND
ENTERTAINMENT
MARKETING

SIMULATION 3

CLIENT: OK Wood

CLASSIFICATION: Skateboard Manufacturer

CLIENT BACKGROUND

In the 1960s, the surfers of Southern California took a sport from Hawaii and created a unique beach lifestyle, influencing music, film, and fashion around the world. The Beach Boys and drive-in movies were the rage, and surf culture was in full swing in the coastal towns of America. Hard-core surfers traveled hundreds of miles just to catch a promising swell.

Unfortunately, however, some days the waves just weren't breaking and surfers were forced to find another way to have fun. It wasn't long before someone had the idea to attach the base of a roller skate to the underside of a plank of wood, creating an entirely new craze: sidewalk surfing.

Otis Keating grew up in one of those coastal towns and began skateboarding when he was five years old. Like his father, Otis became a carpenter by trade. When he was just twenty years old, Otis decided to start his own business. Using his own money and experience at his father's commercial carpentry business, Otis founded OK Wood—a woodworking business specializing in finished cabinetry and furniture making.

As Otis' business grew, so did his woodworking ability. Having never lost his passion for skateboarding, Otis applied his carpentry skills to his creating the perfect skateboard. Whenever he brought a new board home, he would customize it by sawing the tail a little or narrowing the body. About five years ago, Otis began making his own decks. Soon, other skateboarders began requesting his boards.

Otis's love of skateboarding and skills as a woodworker led to success for OK Boards, which has become the principal component of his business. Thanks to an excellent distribution system and a hot Internet site, OK Wood markets its products throughout the United States and the world.

Recently, Otis decided to expand his sales by selling skateboard wheels. The OK Wheel is not revolutionary, but it is light, fast, and top-quality. Researching, designing, and manufacturing the new wheels has been expensive, and OK Wood is counting on immediate financial returns. To do this, Otis is taking business courses at a local junior college to streamline his budget and has contacted Impact! Inc. to review his pricing strategy.

ASSIGNMENT

Enough about Otis, congratulations are in order. At Otis's request, you have been assigned to review and revise pricing for OK Wood's products.

PHASE I PRICING

STEP I

First, help Otis determine the pricing objectives for OK Boards and Wheels. There are four types of pricing objectives:

- ◆ Earn a profit
- ◆ Gain market share
- ◆ Meet the competition
- ◆ Make a return on his investment

Summarize each objective and present your recommendations.

_____

_____

_____

_____

_____

_____

_____

_____

_____

_____

_____

_____

_____

_____

_____

_____

_____

_____

STEP 2

Below is information about the skateboard decks and their total average manufacturing costs:

32" WOOD BOARD $5.00

The Wood Board is designed for basic street tricks on curbs, banks, and mini-ramps. Its compact size and concave shape provide plenty of pop for high ollies and keep the skater's feet in place. It has a 7-layer plywood design and is quite durable.

32" SLICK BOARD $5.50

The Slick Board has all of the advantages of the Wood Board, plus a thin layer of plastic on the bottom for a sturdier stance. It's perfect for rail slides and tricks where concrete will be scraping between the trucks.

42" LONG BOARD WITH TAIL $8.00

The traditional Long Board allows more stability than the Wood and Slick Boards, and features a tail for cruising in style.

48" LONG BOARD WITHOUT TAIL $8.00

The Supercruiser Long Board Without a Tail has maximum support and stability for daring downhill drives.

In the skateboarding industry, the manufacturer typically sells in large quantities to distributors, who then sell in somewhat smaller quantities to retailers, who sell individual items to consumers. The method of pricing is as follows:

Manufacturer to Distributors: 100 percent markup of manufacturing cost
Distributor to Retailers: 100 percent markup of distributor's cost
Retailer to Consumers: 100 percent markup of retailer's cost

Otis wants a report showing the estimated pricing of the four products using the above pricing methods. If you have a computer, use spreadsheet software. If not, copy and complete the spreadsheet below.

PRODUCT	MANUFACTURING COST	DISTRIBUTOR'S COST	RETAILER'S COST	CONSUMER'S COST
32" Wood Board	$5.00			
32" Slick Board	$5.50			
42" Long Board with Tail	$8.00			
48" Long Board without Tail	$8.00			

STEP 3

As mentioned in the client background, OK Wood is expanding its product line to include wheels, which will be available in three sizes: **54mm** (for tricks), **58mm** (for general riding), and **68mm** (for ramps and cruising). Because manufacturing and marketing costs are identical for all three sizes, their prices are identical. The total manufacturing cost for a set of four wheels is $3.

A. Complete another spreadsheet using the pricing formulas below:

Manufacturer to Distributors: 100 percent markup of manufacturing cost
Distributor to Retailers: 100 percent markup of distributor's cost
Retailer to Consumers: 100 percent markup of retailer's cost

PRODUCT	MANUFACTURING COST	DISTRIBUTOR'S COST	RETAILER'S COST	CONSUMER'S COST
54mm Skateboard Wheels	$3.00			
58mm skateboard Wheels	$3.00			
68mm Skateboard Wheels	$3.00			

B. Once the spreadsheet is complete, calculate OK Wood's break-even point on the new wheels. (This is the point at which sales revenue equals the costs of manufacturing and distribution). Otis plans to manufacture 100,000 sets of wheels. How many will he have to sell to distributors to break even? Use the distributor price you calculated in STEP 3A in the following formula:

Distributor's Cost × Number Sold = Manufacturing Cost × Number Made
(Sales Revenue)   (Manufacturing and Distribution Cost)

STEP 1

A. Otis suggests that retailers use the even numbers generated in the chart from Phase 1 as consumer prices. According to odd-even pricing psychology, what does this signify?

_____

_____

_____

_____

B. OK Wood offers the following quantity discounts to distributors:

BOARDS		WHEELS	
50+ boards:	2 percent off price	50+ sets:	2 percent off price
100+ boards:	3 percent off price	100+ sets:	3 percent off price
200+ boards:	5 percent off price	200+ sets:	5 percent off price

Using the spreadsheet below, create a distributor price list that OK Wood can send to its customers. Show the cost of an individual board or case of wheels versus the discounted costs.

PRODUCT	DISTRIBUTOR'S COST	50+	100+	200+
32" Wood Board				
32" Slick Board				
42" Long Board with Tail				
48" Long Board without Tail				
54mm Skateboard Wheels				
58mm skateboard Wheels				
68mm Skateboard Wheels				

IMPACT! *Sports and Entertainment Marketing Mini-Simulations*

C. Jot down a few reasons why OK Wood should or shouldn't use skimming or penetration pricing. (Skimming is setting a very high price for a new product to capitalize on the high demand for it during its introductory period. Penetration pricing sets a very low price for a new product to encourage as many people as possible to buy it.)

_____

_____

_____

_____

_____

_____

_____

_____

STEP 2

A distributor in Japan has ordered 100 sets of wheels, 50—32" Wood Boards, 50—32" Slick Boards and 10—48" Long Boards. What is the total price, excluding tax and shipping? How much does it cost in yen? You can find the current exchange rates in the business section of a newspaper or on the Internet. Since exchange rates fluctuate daily, the invoice should include how the changing rates will affect the yen's value against the U.S. dollar tomorrow.

_____

_____

_____

_____

_____

_____

_____

_____

_____

STEP 1

A. Some of OK Wood's competitors lowered their prices by 5 to 8 percent. Given that its sales are projected to grow by 10 percent this year, should Otis follow suit and change his pricing? Be sure to address the issue of price elasticity in your answer.

_____

_____

_____

_____

_____

_____

B. A few months ago Otis received a call from a competitor trying to convince several companies to raise their prices together. How should Otis respond to the caller? Be sure to consider ethics of price fixing.

_____

_____

_____

_____

_____

_____

C. One of Otis' employees is complaining about a distributor and is proposing that Otis prepare a set of higher prices for this distributor. How should Otis respond to this employee?

_____

_____

_____

_____

_____

_____

STEP 2

To supply Otis with information about his competition, spend some time on the Internet researching at least three competitive sites that sell skateboards and wheels. List the competitors and their prices. If you don't have access to the Internet, look at retailers' ads in the backs of magazines or call some retail shops. Then propose a price list that OK Wood can use to sell directly to customers through the Internet, a toll-free number, or the mail. Of course, the tricky part is to not alienate the retailers who will be competing with this new sales technique. Below the price list, include your thoughts about how OK Wood can accomplish its goals without losing the business of its retailers.

SPORTS AND
ENTERTAINMENT
MARKETING

SIMULATION 4
CLIENT: Torrel Dance Troupe
CLASSIFICATION: Dance Company

CLIENT BACKGROUND

Spain's Torrel Dance Troupe is one of the most famous dance companies in the world. Born and raised in Madrid, Mario was the youngest dancer to have ever become a principal in the Spanish National Ballet Company.

After leaving the Spanish National Ballet Company, Mario wrote a book chronicling his life as a young dancer. The book went to number one on *The New York Times* nonfiction best-seller list. In 1995, he visited New York and Los Angeles on a book-signing tour. Within two days of his arrival in the United States, he signed a deal to star in a motion picture documenting his life. *The Dance of Mario* became one of the top-grossing films of 1996 and catapulted the dancer to international stardom.

Unfortunately, being in the spotlight didn't agree with Mario. The unending routine of interviews, television appearances, and countless parties left little time for Mario to do what he did best—dance. He returned to Madrid and founded the Torrel Troupe in 1997 by teaming up with three local dancers. Today the traveling company features 22 dancers from around the world. The Torrel Troupe has performed for heads of state, at international festivals, and most notably in the opening ceremonies of the 2000 Olympics in Sydney, Australia.

Three years ago, the Torrel Troupe announced its first-ever United States performance in New York. The response was overwhelming, and tickets sold out in minutes. Then, without any explanation, two days prior to the engagement, the troupe canceled. This left ticket holders, patrons of the arts, and New York City in general, angry and upset—vowing never to attend a Torrel performance in the future.

ASSIGNMENT

The Torrel Troupe has just confirmed a three-week limited engagement at Carnegie Hall in New York City. The troupe is hoping to sell out each performance. Impact! Inc. is one of two agencies being considered to promote the event. We've handled tough situations in the past, but nothing like this. If the public perception of the Torrel Troupe doesn't change, it could reflect negatively on Impact! Inc. But, if the engagement is a success, it will be a huge feather in our cap. The success can only come from your superlative promotional plan.

Formulate a proposal to secure the Torrel Troupe account. Each phase of this assignment includes dealing with one aspect of the promotional mix: advertising, publicity, sales promotion, and personal selling. Start by forming a team of four employees and agreeing on (1) who your target market is, and (2) what team member is going to handle which aspect of promotion. Each phase will be handled by a team member. On paper, follow the steps leading up to the group's oral presentation. The final step is a group presentation of the entire team's findings to upper management and to some highly influential art patrons.

PHASE I ADVERTISING

STEP 1

Explain the function of advertising in the promotional mix, and identify how it differs from other forms of promotion.

_____

_____

_____

_____

_____

_____

_____

STEP 2

Develop a list of advertising media and recommend three types to promote the Torrel Troupe. Determine the best media type for the Torrel Troupe, explaining why it is well-suited and how much it will cost. Refer to books, articles, Web sites, or interviews for information. Show your budget on a spreadsheet or on a separate piece of paper.

_____

_____

_____

_____

_____

_____

_____

STEP 3

Identify the skill sets necessary to create your promotion. (For example, will it require illustrators, Web designers, or songwriters?) Referring to trade journals, the Internet, ads, and other sources, provide a list of creative sources. Are any of these sources available in-house?

_____

_____

_____

_____

_____

STEP 4

Will you need to copyright any of the advertising promotions? Research the necessity of copyrighting, and explain your findings.

_____

_____

_____

_____

_____

_____

STEP 5

It's been more than 15 years since Mario Torrel last set foot in the United States. Outline the effect of technology on advertising and how promotion options have expanded over the years.

_____

_____

_____

_____

_____

STEP 6

The Towers Hotel has developed a package to attract out-of-town guests to the Torrel engagement. This package for two includes a two-night stay at the Towers, tickets to the Torrel Troupe performance, and a complimentary pre-show dinner at selected restaurants. The special price for the entire "Weekend Getaway" package is $349. Complete this package by accomplishing the following:

A. Target ten cities for this package. Use a map to determine appropriate distances from New York for weekend getaways—within two to five hours in travel time. Are there other factors in selecting cities?

_____

_____

_____

_____

_____

B. Create an ad for placement in these cities' newspapers. Use a desktop publishing or illustration program if possible. If not, use a separate piece of paper. The ad should include the following elements:

◆ Headline
◆ Illustration
◆ Copy
◆ Signature

STEP 7

Meet with your partners to organize and embellish your "Weekend Getaway" promotion for use in your group presentation.

_____

_____

_____

_____

_____

_____

_____

_____

PHASE 2 PUBLICITY

STEP 1

Start your pitch by defining publicity and summarizing its principal functions.

_____

_____

_____

_____

STEP 2

Define the difference between the publicity and public relations, explaining how one function is controllable and the other is not. Then suggest how to overcome the negative publicity from the Torrel Troupe's last experience in New York. List and elaborate on your ideas to prepare for your presentation.

_____

_____

_____

_____

_____

_____

_____

STEP 3

Investigate how cause-related marketing (linking the product to a good cause, such as charity or the environment) can improve the Torrels' image. Select an appropriate cause and justify it.

_____

_____

_____

_____

_____

_____

STEP 4

Determine and briefly describe five potential public relations and publicity activities for the Torrel Troupe engagement. Choose the best activity and identify, estimate, itemize, and total each of its components. Use a spreadsheet or a separate sheet of paper.

STEP 5

Use a word-processing program to create a news release to inform the media about the Torrel Troupe's engagement at Carnegie Hall. Complete sentences, proper grammar, good spelling, and well-formed paragraphs are imperative because it may appear as is on the radio or in a newspaper. Be sure your release answers the questions who, what, where, when, and why.

STEP 6

Martina Rayden, the director of the Torrel Troupe, suggests that, to counteract some of the bad press, Impact! Inc. falsify information about why the Troupe canceled its engagement three years ago. While you don't want to lie, you also don't want to offend a potential client. How should you respond to Martina?

STEP 7

Meet with your partners to organize and embellish your public relations or publicity promotion (from Step 4) and news release (from Step 5) for use in your group presentation.

PHASE 3 SALES PROMOTION

STEP 1

Briefly explain the objectives of a sales promotion. Outline some unique characteristics associated with it and explain how it differs from the other components of the promotional mix.

_____

_____

_____

_____

_____

_____

STEP 2

Describe at least five sales promotion options available to the Torrel Troupe's engagement at Carnegie Hall. Include a brief paragraph about each activity supporting your decision to use it.

_____

_____

_____

_____

_____

_____

_____

STEP 3

Prepare a paragraph or two describing how licensing works in the promotional mix. Then develop a sales promotion activity for the Torrel Troupe's visit that incorporates licensing. Explain how this idea will encourage sales.

_____

_____

_____

_____

_____

STEP 4

The director of the National Dance Academy here in the United States, an old friend of Mario Torrel from his early days dancing with the Spanish National Ballet Company, wants to coordinate a promotional tie-in with the Torrel Troupe's New York visit. This may be the "in" you need to get the account. Develop a promotional tie-in, and be very clear on how it will boost ticket sales. Design a flyer to promote the tie-in. Use desktop publishing software or a separate sheet of paper. Summarize your tie-in and explain your flyer below.

_____

_____

_____

_____

_____

_____

_____

_____

STEP 5

What types of local businesses might support the Torrel's engagement? Come up with five promotional activities that might get their backing. Remember that both sides need to benefit and it must publicize the Carnegie Hall appearances.

_____

_____

_____

_____

_____

_____

_____

_____

STEP 6

The head of visual merchandising at one of the city's elite department stores may donate a window space to promote the Torrel Troupe's first visit to America. Create, describe, and sketch an attractive promotional display for the space using the elements of visual merchandising. Be sure to consider the artistic elements: line, color, shape, direction, texture, proportion, balance, motion, and lighting. Make sure that your promotional display is consistent with your other sales promotion activities for the Torrels. Sketch the display in the box below and describe the display's merchandise, display setting, artistic elements, and evaluation techniques on the lines that follow.

STEP 7

Select one of the sales promotion activities you've outlined above, and using a spreadsheet program, identify, estimate, itemize, and total each component of that activity. With your partners, work this promotion into your group presentation.

STEP 1

Describe personal selling, contrasting its pros and cons. Then develop a list of personal selling activities that will work well for the Torrel Troupe event. A brief, but detailed description must accompany each activity.

_____

_____

_____

_____

STEP 2

Research the library or the Internet to develop a list of organizations where you can publicize the Torrel Troupe engagement. Include the names and member profiles of the organizations, as well as information regarding how they can help increase ticket sales. Write the information on the table below:

NAME OF GROUP	DESCRIPTION OF MEMBERS	SUITABILITY FOR TROUPE

STEP 3

Use a word-processing program to draft a business letter to the organizations in your database that briefly outlines the Torrel event and requests the opportunity to speak in support of it. Enclose a flyer highlighting the details of the event. To make the flyer, use desktop publishing software or draft a version on a separate sheet of paper. (Make up the the dates and times of the engagement until firm dates are available.)

STEP 4

The steps of selling include approaching the customer, determining needs, presenting the product, overcoming objections, closing the sale, suggestion selling, and customer relationship building. Apply these steps toward developing a sales pitch that promotes the Torrel Troupe to possible ticket buyers. A good first step might be to determine how to reach potential customers and where the personal selling will take place. (Door-to-door? A mall? Telephone marketing?) Describe the details of each step.

_____

_____

_____

_____

_____

_____

_____

_____

_____

_____

_____

_____

STEP 5

Apply the steps of selling to sell Impact! Inc.'s services to the Torrel Troupe. Use the technique to combine each group member's results, organize your group's results, and create a final presentation.

SPORTS AND ENTERTAINMENT MARKETING

SIMULATION 5

CLIENT: Palmer Bicycle Company
CLASSIFICATION: Bicycle Manufacturer

CLIENT BACKGROUND

In 1955, the Baby Boom began, America's suburbs spread, and the Palmer Bicycle Company manufactured its first line of sturdy, dependable bicycles. Located in Wheaton, Wisconsin, the company vowed to put a Palmer bike in every garage—and it came pretty close. Over the next two decades, Palmer's cycles dominated the American bicycle market. By 1975, it had a 37 percent market share and any kid on the street could sing you the catchy "Who doesn't like a Palmer bike?" jingle.

The 1980s saw a dramatic change in the bicycle industry. As the Boomers were growing up, America was swept up in a fitness craze. Cycling wasn't just for kids anymore. It became increasingly popular as a sport. Higher-priced bicycles made from lightweight materials featuring cutting-edge graphics became the industry standard. Palmer's slow response to this changing market resulted in its declining market share that currently stands at 20 percent.

Despite increasing production costs and decreasing sales, Palmer manages to profit by cutting costs and specializing in the lower-end bike market ($75–$200 retail price). Palmer bicycles are primarily sold to the chain discount retailers, where untrained workers perform the assembly function. "Who doesn't like a Palmer bike?" Apparently anyone serious about biking.

Palmer's history in the cycling business, however, is too long to start backpedaling. In an effort to reverse its declining market share, Palmer commissioned a research firm to conduct a study of bicycling. The report concludes:

continued on next page

ASSIGNMENT

Based on the information acquired through the market report, Palmer Bicycle management has stepped up its research and development to broaden its product appeal. Ken Palmer II, CEO of Palmer, has just contracted Impact! Inc. to assist the Palmer R&D department in developing a new line of bicycles that will be lighter, faster, and stronger yet still provide a safe, comfortable ride. Palmer has specified that these bikes retail in the popular $300–$800 range.

Management has assigned you to this account. Form a team along with three other employees. to come up with a slogan and logo for the new product line. Then assign to each team member one component of the promotional mix: **advertising, publicity, sales promotion,** and **personal selling.**

Together, write a marketing plan based on the four Ps of marketing: **price, place, product, promotion.** The final step is a group oral presentation of the entire team's findings and recommendations to the management of Palmer and Impact! Inc.

CLIENT BACKGROUND *(continued)*

◆ The sport of bicycling worldwide has increased significantly over the last ten years and conditions suggest that this increase will continue.

◆ Cycling's growth is driven by several factors: the quest for physical fitness; the twenty-something generation's desire for "life after work"; concerns for a cleaner environment; the increased number of bicycle events including races and tours; and the reality that bicycling crosses all ages.

◆ Two major factors influence the buying decision: (1) how the consumer uses the product (i.e., frequency, off-road vs. paved surface, recreational vs. competitive, etc.) and (2) the bicycle cost.

◆ The largest window of opportunity for bicycle sales today is in the $300–$800 price range. These bikes are typically sold in authorized specialty retail bicycle stores and are assembled by professional bicycle mechanics. This provides a level of safety to the consumer and preserves the product warranty.

◆ The casual bicycle consumer in this price range will most likely ride several times per month on a paved surface or off-road, occasionally venturing into recreational dirt biking, and participating in various fun-ride events.

PHASE I PRODUCT

STEP I

How will you use the new product development process to create a new product line consisting of four bicycles? Remember, the product development process includes the following procedures:

◆ Generate ideas
◆ Screen ideas
◆ Develop the product
◆ Test the product
◆ Introduce the product
◆ Evaluate customer acceptance

Explain how you will accomplish each of these tasks using the information provided in Palmer's background file, your personal knowledge of this sport, and information yielded from research. Be as specific as possible when describing each new bike. Include style, color, features, sizes, materials, and safety considerations. Create bikes that your customers would like to ride.

STEP 2

Determine the brand name for the new line and the model names for each bike in the line.

A. Identify and list the pros and cons of continuing to use the Palmer brand on the new line.

B. Brainstorm a list of other possible brand names.

C. Select your brand name (Palmer or a new one) and include a justification/rationale for using it.

D. Select model names for each of the four bikes in the line.

STEP 3

Develop a brand mark that will appear on the bikes. Use a draw/paint program if possible, or create it by hand in the box below. On the lines that follow, include a written explanation and justification for using this mark.

_____

_____

_____

_____

STEP 4

Meet with your team member in charge of place activities to determine the distribution channels or the new Palmer bike line. Then, describe the elements of packaging, including the following elements:

◆ Size, shape, color, materials, and labeling.
◆ How the assembly of the bicycle (whether it's done by a specialty shop, a discount shop, or at home) affects the warranty.
◆ If recycled materials are used, mention environmentally sound packaging.

STEP 5

Survey warranties provided by other manufacturers in the bicycle industry and then develop one for the new Palmer line. Also create a customer satisfaction survey on the warranty that the customer can detach and return to the manufacturer.

STEP 6

Palmer has gained considerable press by sponsoring bicycle safety seminars. Prepare a bicycle safety tip sheet to include with the consumer manual and distribute at future seminars. Seek out and list at least five potential sources of information on bicycle safety. Is it a good idea to include the Palmer logo in the booklet?

STEP 7

What are some ways Palmer can extend its product mix? Considering accessories, industrial categories, and additional product lines, come up with at least five possibilities.

STEP 8

What are some ways that these new marketing strategies may have to change over the next few years? (Technology, the changing market, and social trends, for example.)

STEP 9

Palmer intends to launch the new line of bicycles in several international markets. Select a non-English speaking country to market your line of bikes. In a paragraph, explain why that country is a potential market. In a second paragraph, describe considerations for marketing the product line in that country. Will it be necessary to change the model names of the bikes?

_____

_____

_____

_____

_____

_____

_____

STEP 10

Palmer's head of Research and Development wants to release a bike made from 100 percent recycled materials. The frame will be made from aluminum cans; tires from recycled tires; hand grips, pedals and other accessories from recycled plastic milk and soda containers; and so on. Write your reaction to the idea of a "Re-cycle" below, including any recommendations for launching such a product.

_____

_____

_____

_____

_____

STEP 11

Use your findings to help your team members write a marketing plan using a word-processor or typewriter. Your team is also responsible for summarizing your findings and recommendations in an oral presentation to the management of Palmer and Impact! Inc.

STEP 1

Identify ten major bicycle manufacturers in the marketplace by searching the Internet, reading cycling publications, visiting bicycle shops, and talking to cyclists. From this list, identify Palmer's direct competitors (i.e., those companies selling bikes with similar features in your price range). Use a database program or the database printout that follows to list the competitors, their models, the features of their products, and how their products compare to Palmer's new bicycles.

MANUFACTURER	MODEL	FEATURES	DO PALMER BIKES HAVE THIS FEATURE?

STEP 2

Compile a list of possible distribution channels and make a recommendation.

A. Create a table that lists the distribution channel members and indicates the pros and cons of each. Include issues of assembly, control, costs, terms, safety, international market connections, and multiple channels. Using word processor file PBP2S2 or a separate sheet of paper, follow the format below:

CHANNEL MEMBERS	BENEFITS	DRAWBACKS

B. After analyzing your chart, select the system(s) you will recommend for Palmer's new bike line. Will an incorrect channel result in problems concerning safety, liability, performance, customer service, or satisfaction? Explain your choice and support your conclusions.

_____

_____

_____

_____

_____

_____

STEP 3

Define the three types of distribution density: intensive, exclusive, and selective. Recommend the type you feel is appropriate for the new line of Palmer bicycles, and identify the factors you considered in your decision-making process.

STEP 4

Discuss inventory control as it relates to the distribution channel, addressing the following:

◆ Why inventory control is important at each segment
◆ Some of the pitfalls of poor inventory control
◆ How technology has changed the inventory control process
◆ Specific inventory control considerations for Palmer (seasonality, new models, etc.)

STEP 5

Meet with your "product" team member to discuss the possibility of marketing the new Palmer bike line in foreign markets. If Palmer exports the line in the country your "product" team member selects, will your distribution channel change? If so, how and why? Explain your conclusions in paragraph form.

STEP 6

Use your findings to help your team members write a marketing plan using a word-processor or typewriter. Your team is also responsible for summarizing your findings and recommendations in an oral presentation to the management of Palmer and Impact! Inc.

STEP 1

There are four types of price objectives:

◆ To earn a profit
◆ To gain market share
◆ To meet the competition
◆ To make a return on investment

Summarize each objective and then recommend one for Palmer Bicycles. Explain your choice.

_____

_____

_____

_____

_____

_____

_____

_____

STEP 2

Research Palmer's competition by going online, visiting bicycle stores, flipping through catalogs, and so on. Find similar models, their selling prices, or manufacturers' suggested selling prices. Summarize your results and determine if these products have elastic demand (a change in price creates a change in demand) or inelastic demand (the price has very little effect on demand)? Explain why.

_____

_____

_____

_____

_____

_____

_____

STEP 6

Create a document for your retailers with a price list showing each bike model, its price, and a manufacturer's suggested retail price (MSRP). Be sure to include any discount information that may be appropriate for that channel member.

_____

_____

_____

_____

_____

_____

STEP 7

Palmer is actively pursuing business in other countries. It has put together a package in which 1,000 of its lowest-priced bicycles from the new series are to be sold for mail delivery in densely populated areas. Choose a country and prepare a competitive bid for it, converting the final bid price to that country's currency using the current exchange rate found in the business section of a newspaper or on the Internet. Also prepare a quote for additional quantities. If the country orders 5,000 units, will the unit price change? Include your answer with the bid, explaining why or why not.

_____

_____

_____

_____

_____

_____

STEP 8

Use your findings to help your team members write a marketing plan using a word-processor or typewriter. Your team is also responsible for summarizing your findings and recommendations in an oral presentation to the management of Palmer and Impact! Inc.

STEP 1

Create an advertising campaign using the following steps:

A. Identify one market segment for the new Palmer Bicycle line and pick an advertising medium for it. Explain Palmer's appeal to the market, and explain why the chosen advertising medium is appropriate.

_____

_____

_____

B. Create an ad for Palmer directed at the selected market segment. Use a desktop publishing or draw program or sketch the ad in the box below. Word process or write on the lines following the box a written explanation identifying each element of the ad (i.e., headline, copy, illustration, and signature) and describe the ad's message.

_____

_____

_____

_____

STEP 2

Create a second ad for a different market demonstrating the use of cooperative advertising.

A. Define cooperative advertising, and explain how it could benefit Palmer.

_____

_____

_____

_____

B. Recommend partner companies for Palmer in this endeavor, and explain why each could benefit Palmer.

_____

_____

_____

_____

_____

_____

STEP 3

If you have Internet access, find at least five different bicycle manufacturer Web sites. (If you do not have access, refer to magazine advertisements of cycling manufacturers.)

A. Critique and summarize what you find. Include likes/dislikes, what was helpful/not helpful, the timeliness of the information, and so on.

_____

_____

_____

_____

_____

_____

_____

B. If Palmer establishes a Web site, what do you recommend it include? What are some potential frequently asked questions (FAQs) that should be answered on the site? Support your suggestions.

_____

_____

_____

_____

_____

STEP 4

Brainstorm a list of at least five PR activities that will benefit Palmer. Organize these activities into a table or database for your report. Include objectives, projected event dates, estimated costs, and other pertinent information. Which activity do you feel is best? Explain your decision in paragraph form.

_____

_____

_____

_____

_____

STEP 5

Use a word-processing program to plan three news releases leading up to the introduction of the new Palmer bike line. Create a timeline for the news releases (explaining why timing is a critical factor) and state what each one will include (spelling out the risk of providing inaccurate information). Be sure to make the content newsworthy. Consider other additions to the press kit.

_____

_____

_____

_____

_____

STEP 6

Palmer's competitors are already trying to sabotage sales of the new high-end bike line by publicizing Palmer's history of manufacturing low-end products. Outline the steps you will take to prepare for this, respond to it, and control it in the future. Will cause-related marketing help? Explain your recommendations.

_____

_____

_____

_____

STEP 7

Brainstorm as many types of trade promotions (slotting allowances, buying allowances, trade shows and conventions, sales incentives) and consumer promotions (licensing, promotional tie-ins, visual merchandising and displays, premiums and incentives, product samples) as you can. Select the ones you will use for the new Palmer Bike line, and justify your reasoning.

_____

_____

_____

_____

STEP 8

Research trade journals and the Internet to create a list of six trade shows and/or conventions in which Palmer should participate. Include all pertinent information such as name of the show, dates, and location. You'll also need to develop a budget for Palmer to attend one of the shows, considering exhibit fees, travel expenses, cost of giveaway items, and so on. If possible, place these in a computer database. Otherwise, write the information below.

_____

_____

_____

_____

_____

STEP 9

Countless sport drink and energy bar companies are looking for tie-in deals with Palmer's new high-end bike line. Palmer hopes to promote an event that demonstrates such a promotional tie-in. This could include a race, a contest, demonstration, etc. Using desktop publishing software or art materials, create a poster announcing the event and highlighting the tie-in between Palmer and the sport drink or energy bar of your choice. The posters will be placed in specialty bike shops to help promote the event.

STEP 10

Draft a sales letter to bicycle store owners requesting a meeting to introduce them and their employees to the new Palmer high-end bike line. Let them know that this meeting will explain the personal selling activities that will promote Palmer's new line and why these activities are critical components of the mix. Spell out why personal selling is a long-term activity that's worth the commitment.

_____

_____

_____

_____

_____

_____

_____

_____

_____

_____

_____

_____

STEP 11

Use your findings to help your team members write a marketing plan using a word-processor or typewriter. Your team is also responsible for summarizing your findings and recommendations in an oral presentation to the management of Palmer and Impact! Inc.

IMPACT! *Sports and Entertainment Marketing Mini-Simulations*

SPORTS AND
ENTERTAINMENT
MARKETING

BACKGROUND FILE

SIMULATION 6
CLIENT: Performances to Please
CLASSIFICATION: Theater Group

CLIENT BACKGROUND

A new theatre group, Performances to Please, has formed in your area. It is planning to present a wide array of programs starring seasoned professionals performing with emerging local talent. The new group is financially sound as it is being backed by a group of well-known creative masters with a history of producing artistically innovative first-class performances. The financial backers own four other award-winning theatre groups with plays currently on Broadway.

As a way of introducing itself to the community, the group approached Impact! with a unique opportunity for a local high school. It has offered to do a series of three performances, donating one-half of the profits from ticket sales to the school for new computer equipment. Your high school has been selected as the recipient of this unique opportunity, and it is now your job to develop a strategy for selling the tickets.

The theatre group wants you to sell tickets not only to parents of the students, but also to other members of the community, including businesses. The three performances will be the musicals: *West Side Story, Oklahoma,* and *The King and I.*

All of these productions are classics that will appeal to a wide segment of the community. Remember, the more tickets you sell, the greater the profit, which means a greater donation to the school for new equipment.

You also have the opportunity to sell ad space in the program, which will help offset printing costs without taking away from ticket sales profit. Therefore it is to your advantage to sell ad space in addition to tickets.

Your contact person at the Performances to Please theatre group is Ms. Jane Sills. She is the President of the group, a past theatre performer, director and

ASSIGNMENT

With a partner, develop a selling strategy for the different performances for which you will be selling tickets and program ad space. Then prepare a two-part presentation that recaps your research and findings on how to sell tickets and ad space successfully and demonstrates an actual selling situation for tickets and ad space. Throughout this project, base your selling strategy on the steps of a sale: approaching the customer, determining needs, presenting the product, overcoming objections, closing the sale, suggestion selling, and relationship building.

CLIENT BACKGROUND *(continued)*

choreographer, a patron of the arts, and a big supporter of public education. Her theatre career spans the past 25 years during which time she directed and choreographed more than 15 major performances with big-name stars. Her most recent productions include *The Will Rogers Follies, Joseph and the Amazing Technicolor Dreamcoat,* and *A Chorus Line.* Ms. Sills comes to your community from the Faye Theatre which was a two-time Tony Award-winning theatre while under her management. Helping her launch this theatre group successfully with your ticket and ad space sales can lead to many, many more opportunities to partner with the group and raise money for much-needed school equipment.

Performances to Please has set established prices for both tickets and ad space sales. Tickets are $21.00 per performance, but the group will allow you to offer incentive pricing packages to help increase both the number and size of the sales. When you create these incentive packages, however, the price is not to go below $17 per ticket.

For selling ad space in the program, the pricing is:

$1/8$ **page = $15.00**
$1/4$ **page = $25.00**
$1/2$ **page = $50.00**
Full page = $100.00

The new theatre group is an exciting addition to your community and offers a wonderful opportunity for your school to acquire new computer equipment. Even though it is almost six months before the first performance, advance planning is critical in this business. So meet with your partner, begin work, and, as they say in the business: "Break a Leg!"

PHASE I PREPARING FOR THE PRESENTATION

STEP I

A. Getting to know your product is an important part of the preapproach. Go to the Internet and research these musicals. For each one, prepare a synopsis of the story, information about who wrote it, its original cast, and when it first appeared on Broadway. Also, identify the memorable songs by title. This research will provide you with background knowledge to help you sell the sizzle!

_____

_____

_____

_____

_____

_____

_____

_____

_____

_____

_____

_____

_____

_____

_____

_____

_____

_____

_____

_____

B Finding customers is the next logical step. Define at least three target market segments for both tickets and ad space in the program. Estimate the size of each target market for your area. Be sure to think ahead and include the sale of ad space wherever possible.

POTENTIAL MARKET SEGMENTS		
TICKETS OR ADS?	**TARGET MARKET**	**ESTIMATED SIZE**
Example: Ad space	All retail businesses within 2 mile-radius of school	40

C. Preparing for the sale is the next step. Document what you should know about each segment, identify what you think are possible buying motives, and indicate what methods of prospecting you will use for each segment.

TARGET MARKET	BUYING MOTIVES	METHODS OF PROSPECTING

STEP 2

Define the service approach, greeting approach, and merchandise approach. Then write an example of an approach to use for each target market segment and explain why you would use the approach.

APPROACH	DEFINITION	EXAMPLE FOR TARGET 1	EXAMPLE FOR TARGET 2	EXAMPLE FOR TARGET 3
SERVICE				
GREETING				
MERCHANDISE				

STEP 3

A. The three methods of determining customer needs are observing, listening, and questioning. For each segment identified above, provide an example of how you might use each method.

TARGET MARKET	OBSERVING	LISTENING	QUESTIONING
SEGMENT 1			
SEGMENT 2			
SEGMENT 3			

B. Develop a list of at least ten questions that you could ask potential customers to help you determine their needs and wants. Again, be sure to include questions geared towards both the ticket sales and ad space sales.

_____

_____

_____

_____

_____

_____

_____

_____

_____

_____

_____

_____

_____

_____

_____

_____

_____

_____

_____

_____

_____

_____

C. Prepare a feature/benefit chart for both the tickets and ad space sales. It must contain at least ten feature/benefit statements.

TICKETS OR ADS	FEATURE	BENEFIT
Example: Tickets	The tickets can be used for different performance dates.	This allows customers with busy schedules more flexibility in planning when to attend.

STEP 4

A. Develop at least three package offerings for both tickets and ad space. Examples may include selling multiple tickets at a discounted rate or offering free tickets to a retailer who buys ad space. You may also want to include premium packages with such activities as "meet the cast," a wine and cheese get-together before the performance, or a take-home souvenir.

_____

_____

_____

_____

_____

_____

_____

_____

_____

_____

_____

_____

_____

_____

_____

_____

_____

B. Using presentation software or art supplies, develop at least three sales aids for use in your selling presentations of tickets and ad space. Examples may include flyers, posters, pamphlets, brochures, ticket mock-ups, props, and order forms.

STEP 5

Prepare an objection analysis chart listing at least two objections (and responses) for each of the general objection categories of **product, price,** and **time.**

CATEGORY	OBJECTION	RESPONSE
PRODUCT	1.	1.
	2.	2.
PRICE	1.	1.
	2.	2.
TIME	1.	1.
	2.	2.

STEP 6

Prepare at least two different dialogs for each product (tickets and ad space) to use in closing the sale. Use a variety of different specialized methods for closing.

_____

_____

_____

_____

_____

_____

_____

_____

_____

_____

_____

_____

STEP 7

Review suggestion selling, and list its five possible uses in this project.

_____

_____

_____

_____

_____

_____

_____

_____

STEP 8

How will you follow up with your customers? List at least eight actions or activities to use after a customer agrees to purchase tickets or ad space.

_____

_____

_____

_____

_____

_____

_____

_____

_____

_____

_____

_____

_____

_____

_____

_____

_____

_____

_____

_____

_____

_____

PHASE 2 DELIVER THE PRESENTATION

Now that you have researched your market and developed your strategies and presentations, it's time to deliver. Ms. Sills just called and wants to meet with you. Using presentation software and sales aids, prepare and deliver a 5–10 minute presentation that provides her with an overview of your research and findings. Then create a selling scenario, and model an actual selling demonstration using the steps of the sale.

PHASE 3 THINKING OUT OF THE BOX ACTIVITIES

STEP 1

Good marketers always think ahead. If your strategy is successful, Performances to Please may want to do more with you. What will you do now to anticipate another campaign to make the sale of tickets and ad space even more beneficial the second time around? How could you develop a system to create a database for future campaigns? How could you use e-mail to communicate efficiently with your customers?

IMPACT! *Sports and Entertainment Marketing Mini-Simulations*

STEP 2

Many live theatre groups nationwide have Internet sites. Go to the Web, research some of these sites, and list the essential elements for a Performances to Please Web site.

_____

_____

_____

_____

_____

_____

_____

_____

_____

_____

STEP 3

Design a system that uses an Excel spreadsheet for tracking and accounting ticket and ad space sales. Should your "first time" customers belong to a "Preferred Members" Club? Why or why not? Will it help your selling dialog?

NAME	ADDRESS	TELEPHONE	FAX	E-MAIL	TICKET PUCHASER	AD SPACE PURCHASER	FIRST TIME CUSTOMER
Example: Bill Jones	12 Main St. San Diego, CA 92111	234-2345	777-1212		Yes or Yes 2 WSS	No	*

STEP 4

Explore the possibility of offering additional merchandise for sale in the lobby before and after the performances. The theatre group will donate 50 percent of the proceeds to your school. What will you sell and why? Will a local supplier donate or offer preferred pricing in exchange for ad space or tickets?

_____

_____

_____

_____

_____

_____

_____

_____

STEP 5

The series of performances was a success! It is important to inform/thank the community for its support. One way is to issue a press release. Write a press release for the local paper. Be sure to indicate the amount of money going to the school for computers, and thank the theatre group for the opportunity.

_____

_____

_____

_____

_____

_____

_____

_____

_____

_____

SPORTS AND ENTERTAINMENT MARKETING INC.

BACKGROUND FILE

SIMULATION 7
CLIENT: Venture Group Limited
CLASSIFICATION: Entrepreneurial Startup

CLIENT BACKGROUND

Today's business community is experiencing an explosion of small entrepreneurial businesses. The sports and entertainment industry is no exception. These small businesses provide the economic foundation of our economy as they continually create additional jobs and offer new and innovative products and services. Most successful entrepreneurs begin their careers by recognizing a business opportunity, starting the business on a small scale, then growing the company.

Impact's client, Venture Group Limited, is a highly successful venture capital organization that finances businesses primarily in the sports and entertainment industry. It provides financial seed and startup funds as well as assistance in the expansions of existing companies. The Venture Group CEO, Phil Cook, has asked Impact! Inc. for a favor. He wants us to provide assistance in organizing a business start-up to Nate Moore, a young man he has known for many years. Though this short-term business is not a typical activity for the Venture Group, Phil is very impressed with Nate and wants to help him get started. Phil truly believes Nate has a great future ahead of him.

Nate Moore is a local 20-year-old man who attends an out-of-state college on a sports scholarship. He is a star player on the college varsity basketball team and has made All-Conference Team the last two years. He is known as a high-energy individual who is disciplined about spending time in the gym improving his basketball skills. He also works hard at achieving top grades in school as a communications major, and carries a 3.5 GPA, which puts him on track to be an Academic All-American athlete.

Nate, who began playing basketball as a young child, loves the game and spends every free moment on the court. He also has an excellent rapport with children. When a group of them wandered onto a court where he was practicing at school one day, it was a natural for Nate to give them tips on their playing skills. At the end of the game, the kids were asking for more, and Nate realized how great

continued on next page

ASSIGNMENT

Evaluate the possibilities of this small business start-up in your community. Then develop a written business plan for Nate. Arrive at a conclusion stating whether or not this is a viable business, and submit supporting documentation for your conclusion.

CLIENT BACKGROUND *(continued)*

it felt to mentor these young players. As a result, he became instrumental in helping a neighborhood youth organization near the college create a highly successful after-school basketball program for children. While working with coaches and other school and community people, Nate has developed a reputation for being highly organized, self-starting, responsible, and confident.

Summer is fast approaching and Nate wants to return home for the break and live with his family, who provide his basic support. With no employment opportunities in sight, and the need to earn spending money, he has decided to do what he does best: begin a business of teaching basketball to children of various age groups by running a series of one-week basketball camps. In these camps, Nate will teach basketball skills and fundamentals. He will be home from college from May 15–September 1, allowing him to operate 12 weeks of camps. He plans to offer two camps a day—one in the morning and one in the afternoon. Each camp will be 3 1/2 hours long for five days, giving a total of 17 1/2 hours of instruction per participant per week. Nate does have some reliable friends from high school who are willing to work in his camps. Nate is not exactly sure how or where he will do this, or even how to get started. So his friend, Phil Cook has asked us to create a business plan to help Nate "get the ball rolling."
(No pun intended!)

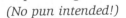

PHASE I PROJECT OVERVIEW

STEP I

Prepare a written list of both the advantages and disadvantages of Nate starting this business. Review it with him to be sure this is what he really wants to do.

ADVANTAGES	DISADVANTAGES

STEP 2

Select a name for this business and provide written justification.

_____

_____

_____

_____

_____

_____

STEP 3

Search the Internet for examples of mission statements, and then write one for this business.

_____

_____

_____

_____

_____

_____

_____

_____

_____

_____

STEP 4

Research the elements of designing an effective business card. Then, using a word-processing/desktop publishing program or art supplies, design a business card for Nate.

The three sections of the business plan will be developed in the following phases and will be combined to create the final business plan. Section 1 is a description and analysis of the proposed business situation. If you have access to a computer, perform the following activities using a word-processing program. Otherwise, write your answers on the lines and in the tables provided.

STEP 1: TYPE OF BUSINESS

Summarize what Nate's basketball camps should include, taking into consideration the information already provided and other items you think will accurately describe the business. Examples include targeted age groups, genders, and activities.

_____

_____

_____

_____

_____

_____

_____

_____

STEP 2: BUSINESS PHILOSOPHY

Write a statement including Nate's philosophy of running a business. Be sure to tie this in with the Mission Statement written above.

_____

_____

_____

_____

_____

_____

_____

_____

STEP 3: PERSONAL ANALYSIS

Prepare a personal description of Nate using the information provided. Identify his key entrepreneurial characteristics, as well as his experience and training in this field. Also, identify what he must do to improve his chance for making this business succeed.

_____

_____

_____

_____

_____

_____

_____

_____

STEP 4: TRADING AREA ANALYSIS

Describe the geographic, demographic, and economic data for the area in your community from which Nate can draw customers. Provide at least a one-paragraph description about each type of data. Sources of information may include your local Chamber of Commerce, State Department of Commerce, real estate offices, census data, or the Internet.

_____

_____

_____

_____

_____

_____

_____

_____

_____

_____

_____

STEP 5: TRADING AREA ANALYSIS

List and describe at least three competitors in the following table. Be sure to include all items that are important to the consumer.

POTENTIAL MARKET SEGMENTS			
ITEMS	**COMPETITOR A**	**COMPETITOR B**	**COMPETITOR C**
NUMBER OF CAMPS			
SERVICES			
AGE GROUPS			
PRICING			
LOCATION			
STRENGTHS			
WEAKNESSES			

STEP 6: MARKET SEGMENT ANALYSIS—TARGET MARKET

Using the information from your research, write a description of the specific group or groups you think are Nate's target markets. Include specific demographic, geographic, and economic information you think is relevant to this business. Examples may include age, gender, income level, family size, population estimate in surrounding area, etc.

_____

_____

_____

_____

_____

_____

_____

_____

_____

_____

STEP 7: MARKET SEGMENT ANALYSIS—BUYING BEHAVIOR

Understanding the buying behavior of the target market will help Nate make many decisions such as how he will reach his market. Identify and list those items that will attract the target market to participate in the camps. Examples include affordability, location, skills taught, etc. Also, think about items like safety, fun, educational aspects, etc.

_____

_____

_____

_____

_____

_____

_____

_____

_____

_____

STEP 8: MARKET SEGMENT ANALYSIS—ANALYSIS OF POTENTIAL LOCATION

Select potential locations for this business and provide a written description along with justification. Consider basic items like safety, access to food and restrooms, traffic, parking, availability, proximity to the target market, and the competition, surrounding noise, and regulations.

_____

_____

_____

_____

_____

_____

_____

_____

STEP 9: MARKET SEGMENT ANALYSIS—ANALYSIS OF POTENTIAL LOCATION

Research how much this location will cost, including rental or lease terms, security deposits, taxes, insurance and maintenance. Prepare a detailed, itemized list of the costs for the Financial Plan.

ITEM	COST

Section 2 of the business plan details the proposed organization of the business. If you have access to a computer, perform the following activities using a word-processing program. Otherwise, write your answers on the lines and in the tables provided.

STEP 1: TYPE OF OWNERSHIP

Indicate what type of ownership Nate should take and why. Consider liability issues, especially when you are working with children.

_____

_____

_____

_____

_____

STEP 2: LICENSES AND REGULATIONS

Identify and list local licenses, fees and regulations that apply to this type of business.

_____

_____

_____

_____

_____

STEP 3: PERSONNEL AND STAFFING NEEDS

Indicate any personnel/staffing needs. Will Nate do everything himself or will he need to hire help? This will depend on the number of children per class, the length of each class, activities, etc. Identify what additional help will be needed, how they will contribute, and how much they will cost. Use the following chart to calculate these costs.

JOB TITLE	JOB DUTIES	HOURS PER WEEK	HOURLY RATE	WEEKLY COST
Example: Assistant	Prepare snacks, help with children	17 ½	$8.00	$140.00

STEP 4: DESCRIPTION OF SERVICES TO BE PROVIDED

Identify the various camp offerings, including the age group for each type. Then develop a daily schedule of the camp activities and a weekly schedule of camp offerings.

_____

_____

_____

_____

_____

_____

_____

See Charts Next Page

DAILY SCHEDULE

TIME	ACTIVITY
Example: 8:00 A.M.–8:15 A.M.	Warm-up exercises

WEEKLY SCHEDULE

WEEK	A.M.	P.M.
Example: No. 1	6–9 year-old beginner	10–14 year-old beginner

STEP 5: EQUIPMENT NEEDED

List all equipment and supplies needed along with their approximate costs. It is important to be thorough and complete. When working with children you have to think of every basic need, like food, water, restroom supplies, medical equipment, etc. It's not just about having basketballs.

ITEM	QUANTITY	COST EACH	TOTAL COST
Example: Basketballs	25	$15.00	$375.00

STEP 6: PROPOSED MARKETING STRATEGIES—PRICING

After analyzing estimated costs, desired profit, and your competitor's pricing, develop pricing for the camp. Consider offering package deals. Examples are discounts for more than one child from a family, attendance at multiple camps, or souvenir basketball merchandise.

STEP 7: PROPOSED MARKETING STRATEGIES—PROMOTION

Think about how Nate will market these camps and what will motivate people to sign up. Identify at least five promotional activities. For example, place posters announcing the camp at local schools, stores, etc. Don't forget about personal selling because Nate has a reputation as an excellent communicator.

Section 3 of the business plan details the financial plan of the business. If you have access to a computer, perform the following activities using a word-processing program. Otherwise, write your answers on the lines and in the tables provided.

STEP 1: SOURCES OF CAPITAL

Because Nate has no personal funds to start his business, Venture Group, Ltd., is loaning him all the start-up money based on his agreement to pay it back in full, plus 5 percent, at the end of the summer. Phil Cook will loan this money as a personal favor to Nate. He has made it clear, however, that this is not the normal mode of operation for Venture Group Limited.

A Personal Financial Statement is generally required to borrow start-up capital. Venture is not requiring a Personal Financial Statement because the owner is a personal friend who realizes that Nate is a college student with no money to invest and is starting a summer business for only three months.

STEP 2: DETERMINING FINANCIAL NEEDS

Determine the total amount of money Nate needs to start the business. Prepare a Start-Up Cost Worksheet beginning with one-time only costs. Refer to the one-time costs you identified in Phase 2. Examples may include licensing, rent deposit, equipment, etc.

ONE-TIME START-UP COSTS	
ITEM	**TOTAL COST**
Example: Licenses	$150.00

STEP 3: DETERMINING FINANCIAL NEEDS

Prepare a worksheet identifying all estimated monthly costs such as salary, taxes, rent, utilities, supplies, etc.

ESTIMATED MONTHLY COSTS

ITEM	JUNE	JULY	AUGUST	TOTALS
Example: Rent	$500.00	$500.00	$500.00	$1500.00

STEP 4: PROJECTED EARNINGS

Estimate income for the three-month period (June, July, August). Consider two camps per week (A.M. and P.M.) and estimate the number of students per camp, and the fee that will be charged.

See Chart Next Page

 Sports and Entertainment Marketing Mini-Simulations

	A.M. # of Students	A.M. Cost per Student	A.M. Total Revenue	P.M. # of Students	P.M. Cost per Student	P.M. Total Revenue	Total Weekly Revenue
Example	15	$125.00	$1875.00	18	$125.00	$2250.00	$4125.00
Week 1							
Week 2							
Week 3							
Week 4							
Week 5							
Week 6							
Week 7							
Week 8							
Week 9							
Week 10							
Week 11							
Week 12							
Totals							

STEP 5: PROJECTED CASH FLOW

Prepare a cash-flow statement showing the money coming into the business for the three months and the money paid out during that time. For the costs, income and expenses, use the information that you calculated in previous sections.

	JUNE	JULY	AUGUST	TOTAL
Beginning of Month:				
Beginning Cash				
Less Start-up Costs				
TOTAL BEGINNING CASH				
TOTAL MONTHLY INCOME				
EXPENSES:				
TOTAL EXPENSES:				
Net Cash Flow				
Cash Surplus (or Need)				

IMPACT! *Sports and Entertainment Marketing Mini-Simulations*

Provide a written recommendation that summarizes the viability of this business. Cite your research and how it supports your conclusion. If you have access to a computer, write your conclusion using a word-processing program. Otherwise, write your conclusion on the lines provided.

_____

_____

_____

_____

_____

_____

_____

_____

_____

_____

_____

_____

_____

_____

_____

_____

_____

_____

_____

_____

_____

_____

NOTES

NOTES

NOTES

NOTES

NOTES

NOTES

NOTES

DATE DUE

JUL 0 5 2010			
JUN 2 8 REC'D			
DEC 1 5 2010			
MAR 1 8 20			
GAYLORD			PRINTED IN U.S.A.